COLLAGE this JOURNAL

For Emily

Potter Style

THis bOok Belongs to

COLLAGE your NAMEHERE ↑

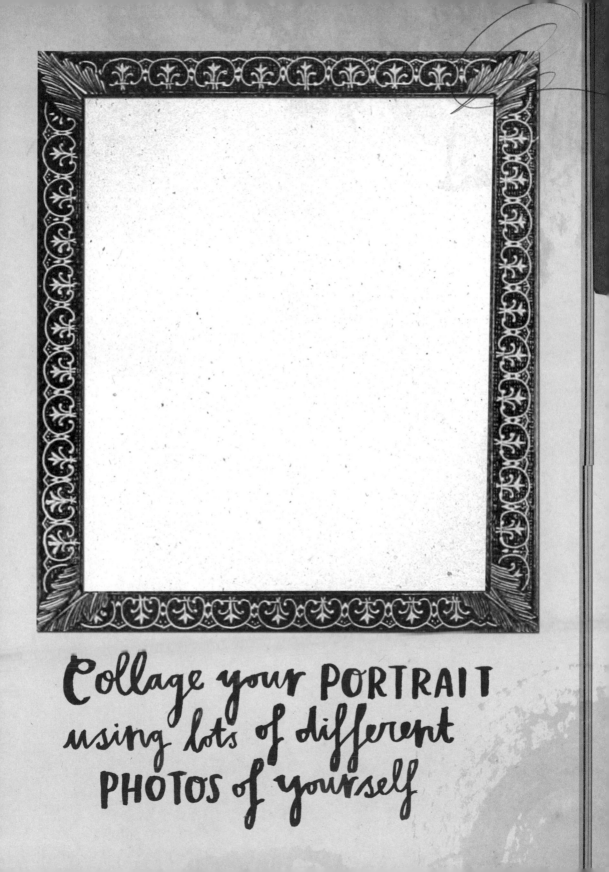

Collage your PORTRAIT using lots of different PHOTOS of yourself

Collage this Journal contains fifty-two projects for you to CREATE your own visual DIARY.

Respond to the projects in an order that feels best for you, completing ONE at a time or doing multiple activities at once.

Your response TODAY may be different from TOMORROW, so however you choose to CREATE, it will reflect your personal JOURNEY. Above all, enjoy!

The Basic Principles of COLLAGE

PHOTOCOPY material to avoid **DESTROYING** the original, **ESPECIALLY** precious things like old photographs.

COMBINE photographic and collage elements with sketching and taking notes.

Photograph items you want to include and print them out.

Use a strong GLUE STICK.
Cheaper ones will come
unstuck eventually.

◆◆◆◆◆◆◆◆◆◆◆◆

To start your own collection of
EPHEMERA, keep your eyes peeled
in thrift shops and
flea markets, as well as online.

◆◆◆◆◆◆◆◆◆◆◆◆

Get a good craft knife and REPLACE
your blade REGULARLY.
If you need to cut through a page,
slide a CUTTING MAT behind it first.

Do you ever wish you could BOTTLE a MOMENT?

What would fall out of your TIME CAPSULE in 100 years?

Tell the STORY of your favorite RECORD

Create falling LEAF shapes of THINGS you want to LEAVE behind

leave

HERE

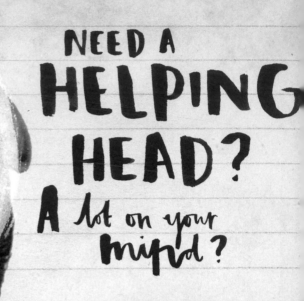

What does the FUTURE hold for you?

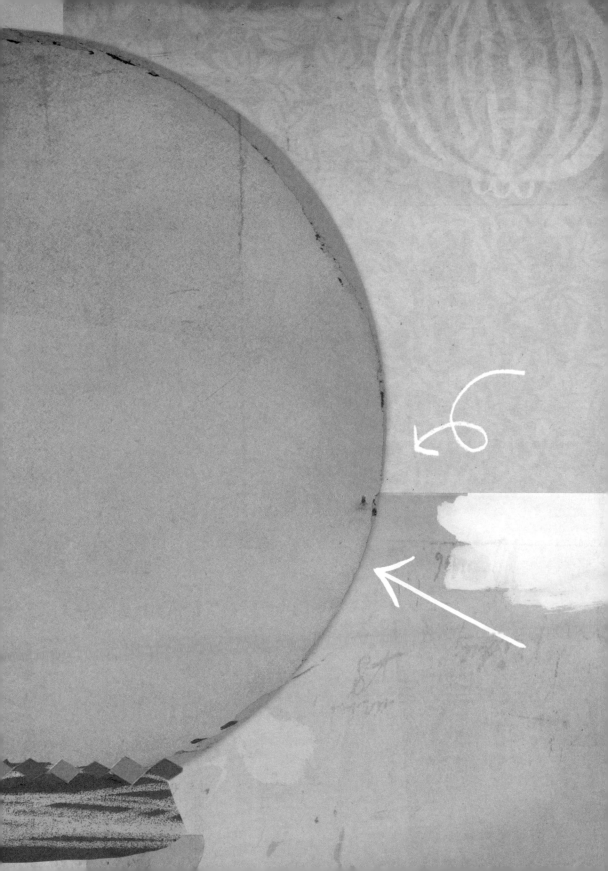

Fill the CABINET full of things that you are CURIOUS about

When you were YOUNGER
what did you want to be?

And how about NOW?

II.2

No.
And
LUCIO

ANGE
You
And
ISABE
Why
And
Fou
If H
But
And
Like
ANGE
—It is
Wer
It sh
ISABE
Ton
He's
We
With
To
Who
Then
LUCIO
ANGE
The
Thos
If th
Had

Fill the frames with photos of FRIENDS and FAMILY

Create your perfect VIEW

Plant things you want
to see GROW in your LIFE

Fill the scales with things that hold particular WEIGHT or significance in your life

COLLAGE yourself as a SUPERHERO

What would your POWERS be?

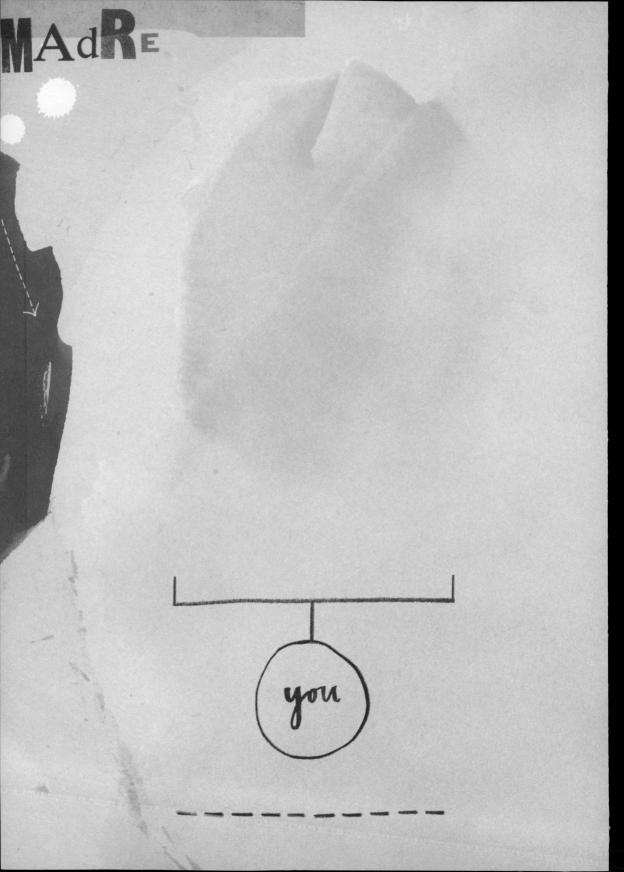

Create your own FAMILY TREE

FRÈre

WHAT PATH ARE YOU ON?

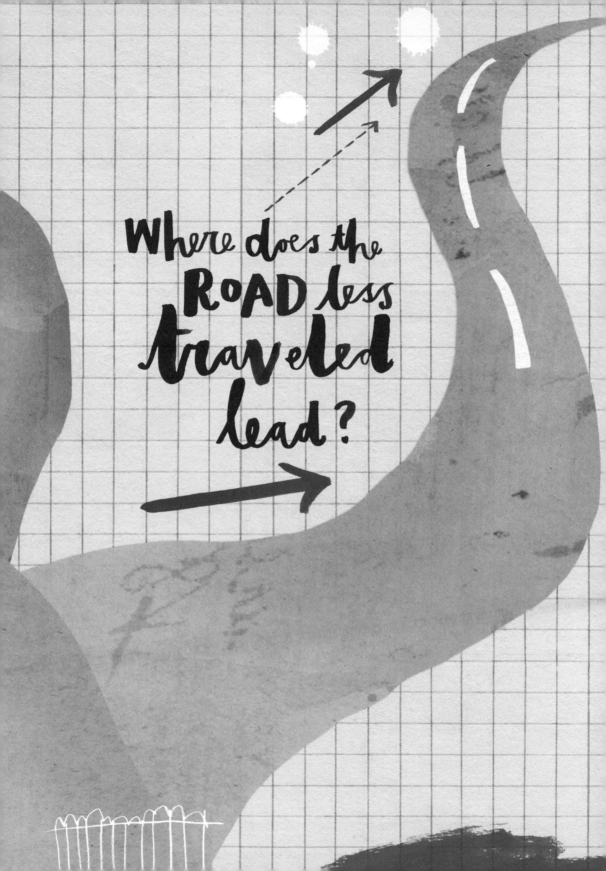

Who or what are your major HANG-UPS?

Create your own
TINY WORLD

Fill the page with BRIGHT IDEAS

REDESIGN
the covers of
your favorite BOOKS

Who would get an INVITATION to your ultimate DINNER PARTY?

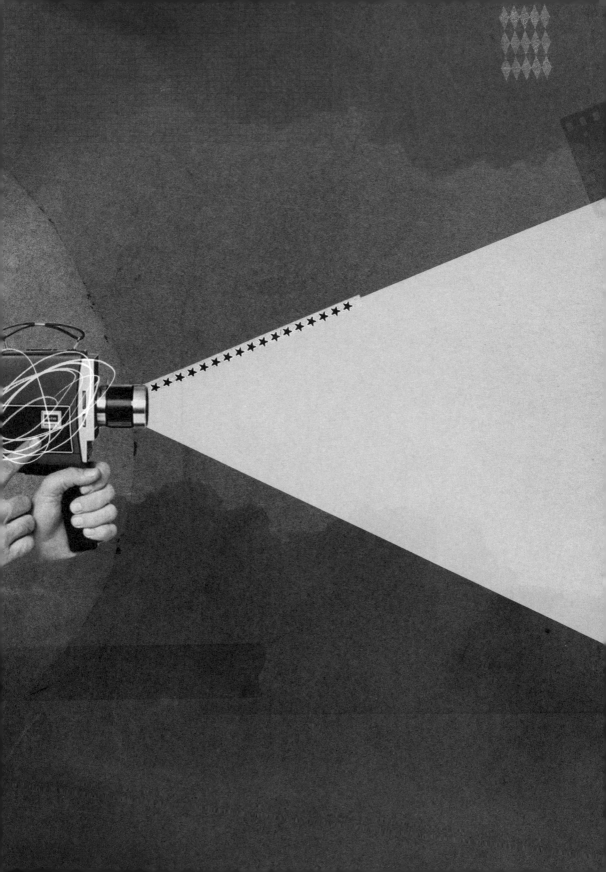

Collage
a home VIDEO of
your happiest
memories

Make a PATCHWORK collage

collected from

quilt using ephemera your
friends and family

Fill this room with your FEARS, PHOBIAS, and things you HATE

Create signs using good ADVICE you've received

BE KiND

reLaX

How would you use a bit more TIME?

What NOURISHES you?

mmm...

CREATE FOOTPRINTS

using photos of places you've been

YOU

How much do you have
in Common?

THEM

Fill this page with THINGS that are your FAVORITE COLOR _ _ _ _ _ _ _ _ _ _

Collage your three GREATEST achievements!

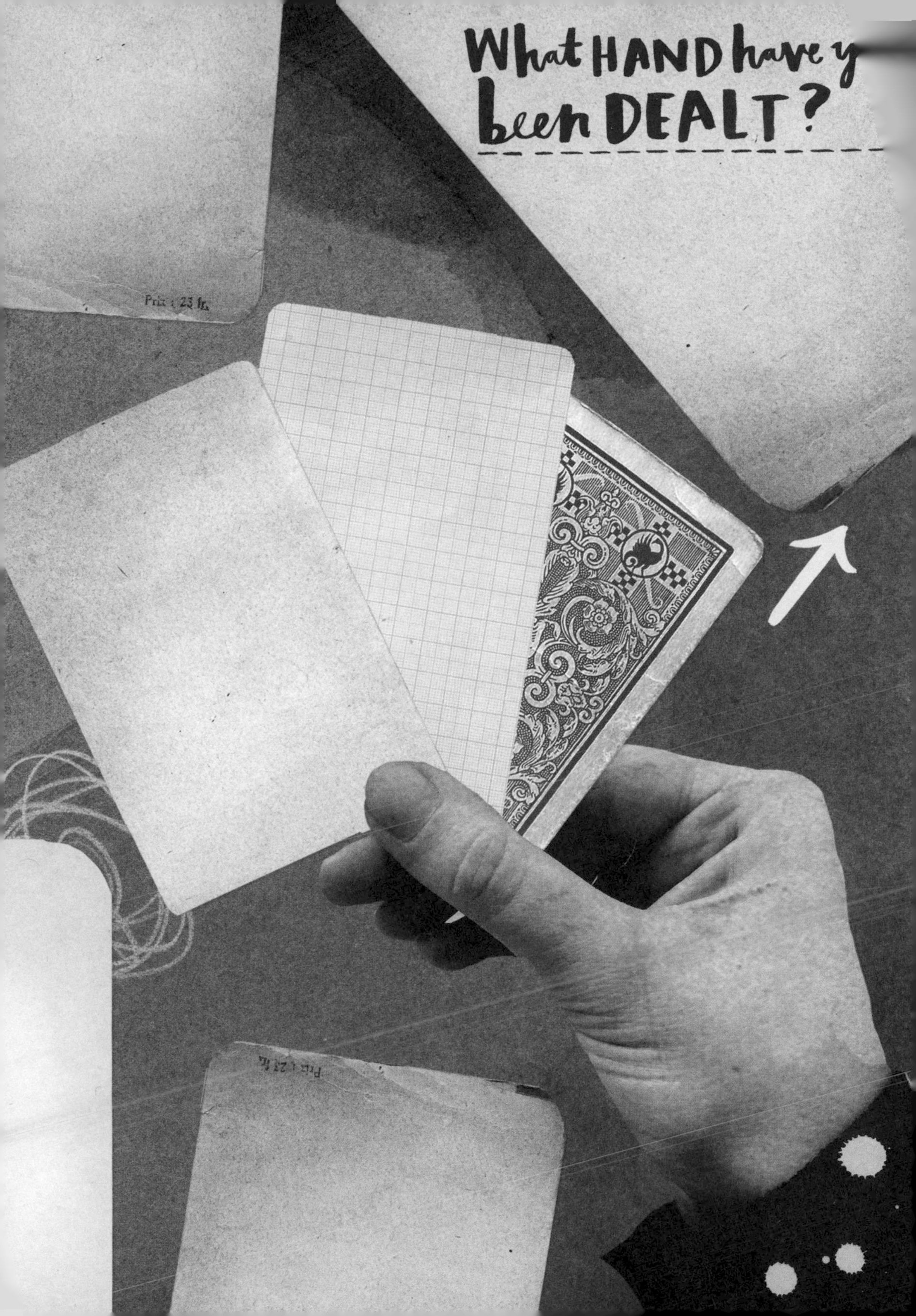
What HAND have y
been DEALT?
Prix : 23 fr.

Collage a PAPER CHAIN of people you connect with

Collage key events from your life to show your JOURNEY

What are your **GOOD** HABITS?

What are your BAD HABITS?

Who or what do you

Collage your favorite Looks

Who or
What makes
your HEART
SING?

w did *you*
see the
WORLD as
a child?

THEN

NOW

How do you see the WORLD now?

Collage SECRET THINGS on these pages, and then sew them SHUT

What makes you COLD?

What makes *you*
HOT ?

Pack ONLY
your most
treasured
possessions
for the
DESERT ISLAND

Make balloons
out of photos from
SPECIAL and
HAPPY occasions

se photos to DOCUMENT how
you have changed over TIME

If you were **WORLD** LEADER for a day, what would **you** CHANGE?

What do you see when

you look in the MIRROR?

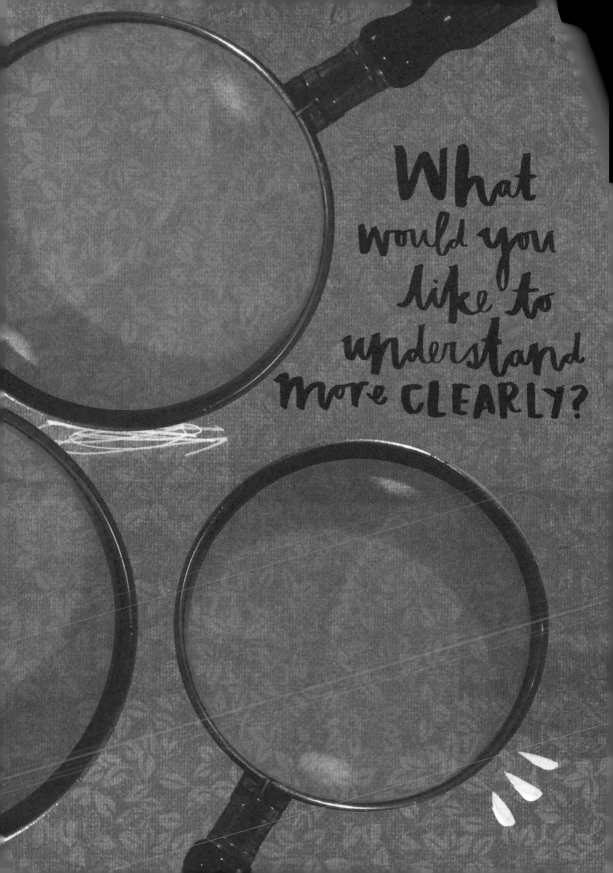

PAREGORIC

What makes you

Create a secret DEN

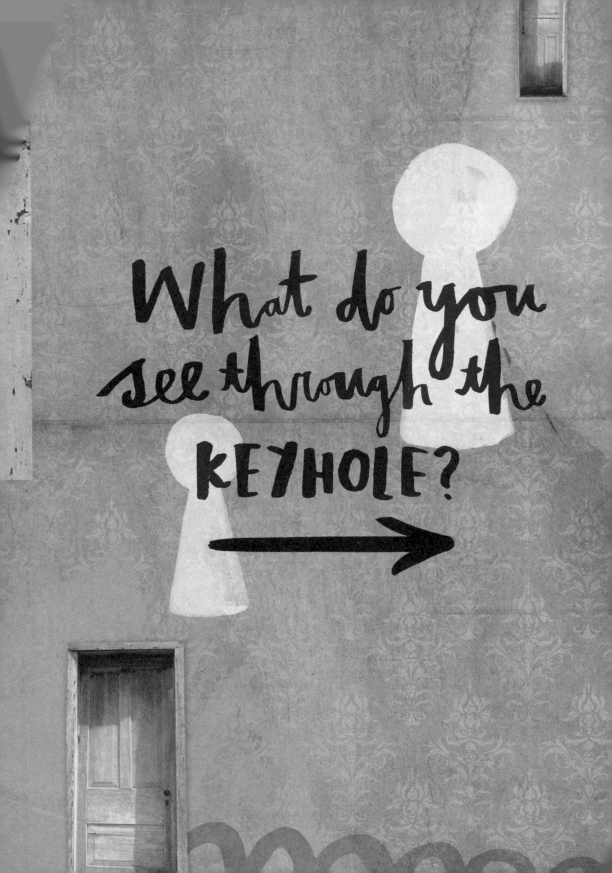

THANK you so so so much:

To my agent, SURESH, whose patience and perseverance know no bounds

To my EDITOR, Nicki, and the whole team at FRANCES LINCOLN, whose vision and passion for this book made it possible.

To Mum and Dad, James and Olivia, my wonderful grandparents, and my extended family for your continued love and support

To Rachel for your brilliant mind

To Chris, Jonathan, Gary, and Phil at The University of the West of England. I owe you so much

To Brittany and the boys in Bristol

To Alex, Duncan, Abbie, and all my friends and colleagues at Greenshaw High School

To my family at Carshalton Beeches Baptist Church

5

Copyright © 2015 by Frances Lincoln Limited
Text and artwork copyright © 2015 by Eleanor Shakespeare

All rights reserved.
Published in the United States by Potter Style, an imprint of the Crown Publishing Group,
a division of Penguin Random House LLC, New York.
www.crownpublishing.com
www.potterstyle.com

POTTER STYLE and colophon are registered trademarks of Penguin Random House LLC.

Originally published in the United Kingdom by Frances Lincoln Limited, London, in 2015.

Library of Congress Cataloging-in-Publication Data is available upon request.

ISBN 978-1-101-90533-3

Printed in China

10 9 8 7 6 5 4 3 2 1

First U.S. Edition